THE HUDSON SOUND
VINYL CITY MUSIC MAKERS

ABRAHAM J. SANTIAGO

HARBINGER PRESS

OTHER BOOKS BY ABRAHAM J. SANTIAGO

Acappella Street Corner Vocal Groups
A Brief History and Discography of 1960s Singing Groups
with -Steven J. Dunham

The Untold Story- United Group Harmony Association

Acappella Living in the Shadows 1963-1973 A Social History

Acappella Viviendo En Las Sombras 1963-1973 Una Historia Social

HARBINGER PRESS
THE HUDSON SOUND- VINYL CITY MUSIC MAKERS by Abraham J. Santiago
Harbinger Press 400 Greenbay Rd #105 Glencoe, IL 60022 USA
Latin American address: P.O. Box 126 Guaynabo, Puerto Rico 00970-0126
Email: msproductions66@yahoo.com

Printed in the United States of America. All rights reserved. No part of this book may be reproduced or transmitted in any form or by any means, electronic or mechanical, including photocopying, recording, or by an information storage and retrieval system-except by reviewer who may quote brief passages in a review to be printed in a magazine, newspaper, or on the web-without permission in writing from the publisher or author. Although the author and the publisher have made every effort to ensure the accuracy and completeness of information contained in this book, we assume no responsibility for errors, inaccuracies, omissions, or any inconsistency herein. Any slights of people, places, or organizations are unintentional.

Copyright 2019-5779 by Abraham J. Santiago
All rights reserved

Printed and bound in the United States of America
Create Space Independent Publishing Platform
Santiago, Abraham J.

ISBN- 9781798658796
Library of Congress Cataloging-in-Publication Data

First Edition 2019
Contains bibliography and index
Doo-Wop-Music- United States-History and Criticism

ACKNOWLEDGEMENTS

I would like to express my deep appreciation to all historians, authors, vocal group singers, journalist, universities, colleges, radio personalities, recording engineers, web sites, clubs, record shops, and organizations that have promoted the R&B group sound and specifically acappella. I deeply appreciate everyone's devotion and commitment to advancing group harmony singing. I want to thank past and present individuals who were there for me and a source of encouragement in this endeavor. I realize that I may have missed some people and I do apologize. I want to thank Jersey City Public Library, Northwestern University, Jon Rich, Bob Davis, Maurice Kitchen, Julie Hurwitz, Jerry Lawson, Daniel Muraida, Charlie and Pam Horner, Wayne Stierle, Steven J. Dunham, Tommy Mitchel, Joe Calamito, Frederick J. Amoroso Jr, Kenneth Banks, Lawrence Pitilli, Edwin Rivera, Juan Perez, Jimmy Merchant, George Scott, Glen Fisher, Mike Miller, Val Shively, Richard and Marie Orisak, Patricia Meidel, Jim De Rogatis, University of Puerto Rico, Doo-Wop/Oldies Forum.

DEDICATED TO MY PARENTS

ABRAHAM AND JOSEFA SANTIAGO

Honor thy father and thy mother, as the Lord thy God hath commanded thee

Deuteronomy 5:16

And

MY FATHER-IN-LAW OF BLESSED MEMORY

SAMUEL LOME

And he hath filled him with the spirit of God, in wisdom, in understanding, and in knowledge, and in all manner of workmanship

Exodus 35:31

CONTENTS

Acknowledgements V
Introduction ix

Part One: Musical Styles 1
    Chapter One: The Power Of Music 2

Part Two: The Way It Was 15
    Chapter Two: The Emergence Of A New Sound 16

Part Three: Social Boundaries 51
    Chapter Three: High School Days 52

Part Four: High School Romance 55
    Chapter Four: The Ferrissian Connection 56
    Ferris High School 62

Part Five: Our Vinyl Records 71
    Chapter Five: Pioneer Acappella Record Labels 72

Part Six: Reflection 103
    Chapter Six: Something To Think About 104
Work Cited 113
About The Author 118
Appendix: Harmony With God 119
Index 123

INTRODUCTION

For some time now, I've been thinking about the classification, and birth of musical regional sounds across America. I have seen very little, if any, an in-depth explanation regarding these regional sounds and there are many such sounds. For some reason, those who created, shaped, and fashioned regional genre sounds have failed to explain how the sound was formed, why it was special, and how it was different from other sounds. This tome or work, is about a musical sound that appeared in the 1960s of which music historians seem to have no memory. It is about a type and specific sound that came from a certain classification. It is part of the family tree of rhythm and blues. It is a musical sound that gave birth to something different and unique. This sound provided the genetic code to urban communities that stretched from Boston to Philadelphia. This book is an attempt to introduce, reveal, and describe a vocal style that has been suppressed by historians for over five decades. It is my hope that this work will elevate the human voice to its rightful place of group singing. This book is about street corner vocal groups who sing in the *acappella* style. There has been no qualitative or quantitative research to date on this subject. Steven J. Dunham and I produced our first book addressing the topic of acappella street corner singing in 2006. In that book, we provided a brief historical outline of the period and furnished a complete discography of all known acappella commercial recordings. Additionally, we provided photos of acappella singing groups, and contributed short biographical sketches of these groups. When we began that project, there was no point of reference, as no one had yet written about acappella as an urban pop genre.

We were the first to compile interviews of former acappella group members of the 1960s. In addition, we interviewed record producers of acappella record labels. Moreover, we studied and analyzed the recordings they made. Lastly, we compiled a brief social, cultural, and historical narrative that traced the emergence of the acappella genre. We were the very first pioneers to introduce this historical musical genre in our first book, *Acappella Street Corner Vocal Groups: A Brief History and Discography of 1960s Singing Groups.* This work was followed by the very first documentary film about acappella, *Street Corner Harmony,* which was a nominee for Best Documentary Film at the Golden Door International Film Festival in Jersey City, New Jersey in 2011. My latest book, *Acappella Living in the Shadows 1963-1973: A Social History* has been used as a template and reference point for students, scholars, and those who want to study the genre. I hope that many others will come forward and write about this genre. I believe that this field is worth studying and exploring. For decades, there has been a historical obfuscation of this class of music on the part of historians. This venture will divulge what took place years ago, and will correctly place its contribution in history.

The groundwork has been laid, and now it's up to serious scholars to take the mantel, move forward, and investigate further. From 1963 to 1973, a new sound emerged in urban America. This new sound metastasized and grew larger than life. There were no advocates or leaders who officially promoted this new genre and sound. There were no leaders like those of the Civil Rights Movement who introduced the potential merits of their mission. The only voices were those of the singers. These singers came from poor and working-class neighborhoods in a time of racial and ethnic tension.

They came from African-American, Jewish, Italian, Puerto Rican, Irish, and other ethnic groups. No one spoke for them or promoted their music, as others did in the Civil Rights Movement, or student activists who protested the war. These singers did it themselves—with their own voices. The songs they sang, the commercial recordings they produced, and the shows they performed spoke for them. In a sense, they created their own Vinyl City where they entered a new dimension of sight and sound. Their Vinyl City was composed of layers of different colors, like humanity, resembling our vinyl records. It should be noted that some parts of this work appeared in my previous books with some alterations. My objective is to promote our unique style to the public and to music historians. I believe that I have made a strong case in introducing this classification as a regional pop brand. It is time now to uncover what happened musically behind the scenes. This book is about their voices and the new musical sound they created. It is a journey of music makers who carved out a niche in the music world. It is their story and their voice—a true story that's never been told.

In perfect harmony,
Abraham J. Santiago

PART ONE

MUSICAL STYLES

CHAPTER ONE

THE POWER OF MUSIC

During the 1960s, a social, cultural, and spiritual upheaval in American society took place. Music became a channel of expressing social conditions of the time, as well as conveying different musical styles. Music was a powerful force for change, much like social media today. The music of the 1960s and early 70s contained elements of urban, regional, and country music, and a little bit of everything else in between. Musicians and singers vented frustration, spirituality, sex, love, and peace. One could say it was a time when music was simultaneously experimental and creative. Music communicated a message to young people and connected us to those we wanted to influence—much like Facebook, and other social media outlets do today. As a matter of fact, this was probably the most creative period in the history of American music. The musical culture at this time even created a distinct style of dress, language, and behavior through musical genres. This demonstrated the power of both music and singers, who sought to lift the mundane lives of others to be more meaningful and purposeful.

Let us begin by briefly identifying some of the regional sounds that evolved during this period. This will help us to understand in context the arguments presented in this book. The terms "musical sounds" and "regional sounds" will be used interchangeably here, because many of these sounds originated in certain geographic areas of the United States. The region from which a musician came from was often expressed through their cultural world view, culinary taste, religious expression, fashion, and political ideology. One can easily see these expressions as one travels across America from coast to coast. America is a multi-layered country with different veneers and textures. This is true not only in regards to culture, but also to race, ethnicity, and music. One need not travel far to experience the diverse tapestry of America. With this said, let us review a few examples of these sounds from the social-cultural revolution of the 1960s. Perhaps one of the best examples is found in *Psychedelic Rock,* which became popular during the mid-1960s with its own sound, cultural ethos, art, and fashion. Psychedelic Rock was a hippie counter-culture musical style that expressed itself through hallucinogenic drugs and other mind-inducing chemicals. San Francisco, California was the breeding ground of this genre, and the city became a focal point for young people who believed that they could make a difference in the world by playing music, getting high, and having spontaneous sex. Young people looking for love and peace made the pilgrimage to Haight Ashbury, a psychedelic neighborhood of San Francisco. The neighborhood was a gathering place for flower children, non-conformists, and activists with anti-establishment views.

Against this background, this type of music became the epicenter of a new regional sound in northern California. This new and provincial musical sound is best known among bands such as Jefferson Airplane, Big Brother and the Holding Company, and Cream. Another regional sound came from the same state. The *Surfing Sound,* introduced by the Beach Boys, depicted music with roaring waves, seagulls, beautiful girls, and surfing. The surf sound attracted thousands of young people to sunny southern California to pick up girls, freeload, party, and race speed cars. This style of music was addictive to young people, and many families moved West as a result of the cultural shift. The attire of those involved in the genre was loosely-fitted casual clothes like shorts, bathing suits, and sunglasses, a style that is de rigueur in southern California. Another class of singers created their own genre style that is similar in nature to the southern Californian style. The Carpenters, The Mamas & the Papas, The Associations, and others created the *Sunshine Pop* genre. This new musical sound was rooted in easy living and easy listening, and emphasized the beauty of the world.[1] Some have even included the 5th Dimensions with this group, while others classify the group as *Champagne Pop* because of their mélange of soul, jazz, Broadway hits, and R&B.

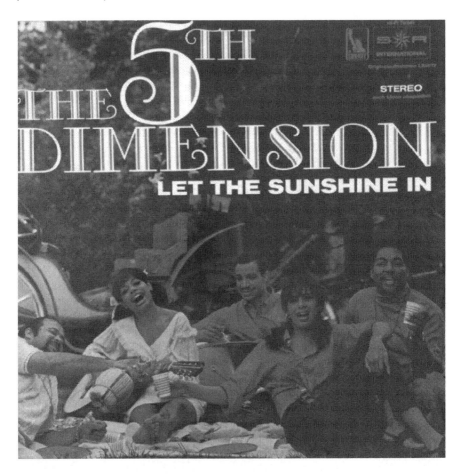

---

1 https://music.avclub.com/sunshine-pop-1798225095

Flower Children
(Courtesy of *Life Magazine*)

In contrast to the robust psychedelic rock sound of San Francisco and the surfing sound of southern California is the *Chicago Sound* of Illinois. This musical style was suave, soulful, and a distinct sound that expressed itself among black and white youth living in the city. The sound of Chicago was an explosion of soul music with many record labels such as Mar-V-lus, Okeh, Chess, and Vee Jay. The Chicago Sound was personified by Curtis Mayfield, Jerry Butler, and groups like The Impressions, Chi-Lites, and Dells. Moreover, Chicago was also the epicenter of *Blues* with artist like Muddy Waters, Buddy Guy, Bo Diddley and many others. Every year it would host its summer festival of Blues, and thousands of people from all over the world would converge to hear, eat and groove. Chicago was the musical engine of the Midwest from doo -wop, blues, jazz, soul and everything in-between. It was Motown, however, that stole the show from the top producing record company in Chicago—Brunswick Records, which was led by Carl Davis at the time. The Chicago sound was the most prominent sound of the Midwest until Motown came on the scene.

The founder of Motown was the legendry self-made millionaire Berry Gordy, whose wealth grew through a company he started with only $800.00. His insight into music, his persistence in accomplishing his goal, and his clear objective made his record company a major contender in the record industry. His company produced entertainers who were sharp, well-groomed, and disciplined singers and musicians. The label's house band, the Funk Band, was the power behind their success, and the band produced hit after hit, producing songs with an urban regional sound that blossomed into a nation-wide and international sounds. Their style of music became an international brand. The musicians of the Funk Band were seasoned Jazz players, and were renowned for their improvisational skill. With the help of the Funk Band, the Motown writers became the sound of young America, and were often portrayed as such to the public. One writer who contributed much to the success of Motown was Smokey Robinson. His group The Miracles, along with others, prodigiously produced musical hits that cemented Motown as the musical powerhouse of the Midwest.

While many regional sounds pounded the airwaves, drawing in young people, Motown became a prominent force. As an urban regional genre of the Midwest, Motown competed with many record companies and artists. One record company that gave Motown a competitive survival edge was a small, independent record company. During this time, a new sound emerged that competed with the Midwest sound of Motown. This new sound came from the city of Memphis, Tennessee, via Stax Records. Stax Records had its own its own raw, gritty, and soulful sound that captured the emotions of the singers, and transferred that sound to its listeners. This was known as *The Memphis Sound*, and it drew millions to a new soul groove fusion that was different from the urban sound coming from Detroit. Otis Redding exemplified the Memphis sound with his gritty, soulful sound that put Memphis on the map as a southern regional powerhouse. His signature song, "*Sitting on the Dock of the Bay*," was a major hit before his untimely death. Also, in this genre were Booker T and the M. G.'s mellow, hip, grooving song "*Green Onions*." In addition, there were Sam Moore and Dave Prater with their hit "*Hold on I'm Coming*," which personified the Stax Memphis sound. These regional sounds from the West Coast, the Mid-West, and the South gave meaning and purpose to young peoples' lives. It transported them from the mundane to a different dimension. In cities like New York, various genre sounds dominated the airwaves, driving people to shows and concerts. A case in point is the birth of Salsa. Salsa was a Latino barrio sound introduced by Fania Records, which came into existence around 1963. One could say that the pioneers of Salsa or Latin Soul were Johnny Pacheco and Jerry Masucci, whose music became a global brand. Their genre captured the hearts of Latinos on the Atlantic coast who were living in the barrios while they were being exposed to Motown, Philla Sound, and other soulful grooves. The Fania label was similar to Motown in that it was a powerhouse Latin record label from New York City that made everyone dance and groove. Goldman writes:

Fania was an unprecedented financial engine, exporting Boricua and Nuyorican culture all over the world. The label held what musician and ethnomusicographer Christopher Washburne calls a "monopoly on all aspects of the salsa industry," controlling "recording contracts, concert promotion, and radio airplay."[2]

People like Johnny Pacheco, Eddie Palmieri, Willie Colon and others got people dancing in the streets on hot summer nights when the fire hydrants were open and water flowed down the streets. One of the great musicians and leaders of the Latino conclave was the beloved pianist Larry Harlow, who was part of that great assembly of promoting Salsa. His legendary piano style and compositions brought Salsa to the forefront. This Latin Jewish brother's influence on Salsa made him a legend and a prince among Latinos. The new Salsa groove that came out of the barrio in Spanish Harlem gave Latinos a new identity. Salsa became a new genre sound—a vinyl groove that gave people something to dance to, and something to focus on.

For people living in a confusing and sometimes hostile world, for people hungry and desperate for a voice — Salsa became that voice. For younger people, who lived in two cultures — one at home and another on the street — it was a bridge between the two, and a generational bridge, bringing several generations of Latinos together with its welcoming and irresistible sound.[3]

We must not forget that by this time there existed reputable musical sounds in many places, and that many local sounds were growing in popularity. Music such as the bluegrass coming from Charleston, West Virginia had a unique cultural ethos. The same could be said of the artistic jazz of New Orleans.

We can see that many regional areas within America had a unique and

---

2 https://www.theparisreview.org/blog/2014/10/09/cha-cha-with-a-backbeat/
3 http://www.pbs.org/wgbh/latinmusicusa/legends/fania-all-stars-and-johnny-pacheco/

established musical reputation. Some areas of the United States produced a mixture of musical categories. A number of song writers, musicians, and singers put certain states on the map and drew thousands of tourists to the state. For example, John Denver's hit song *"Take Me Home, Country Roads"* was released in 1971, and drew thousands of tourists to the state of West Virginia, boosting the regional economy.

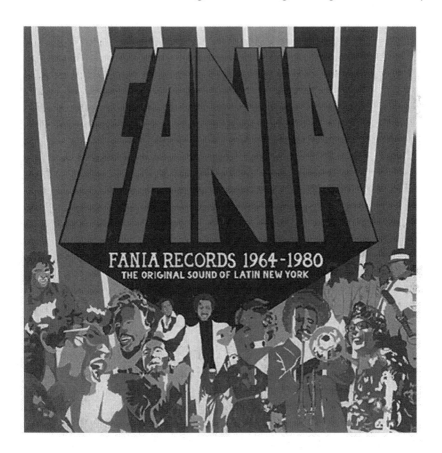

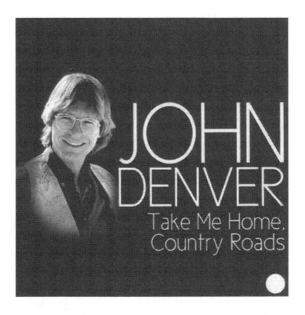

Let us not forget the *Folk Sound*, which was popular during the period on college campuses, coffee shops, public parks, and among upper-middle-class young people. The music drew thousands of people to open-air concerts, stadiums, TV channels, and radio stations, and swayed America with simple guitar and harmonic vocals. One of the of trailblazers of this genre was the trio of Peter, Paul, and Mary, whose signature song *"If I Had a Hammer"* was a major hit when so many songs, vocal bands, soloists, and other vocal groups were hammering the pavement to make their own songs a hit. There was also the New Christy Minstrels, directed by Randy Sparks, with their hit *"This Land is Your Land."*

Some folk singers did not represent a regional area, such as Judy Collins with her hit song *"Both Sides Now,"* which was released in 1968, which combined folk and pop genres. Regional sounds played an important part in molding America's musical palate and bringing people together. All the above musical styles, with their heartfelt sounds of life, were communicated by singers, songwriters, and musicians. What social media represents today in terms of bringing people together and informing them of cultural phenomena, so was music during that period of the

1960s and 1970s. In a sense, music was the social media of the 1960s and 70s. Vinyl records were played on the radio, in homes, and in public places, and as such, had a tremendous impact on young people.

One regional sound emerged within this multi-faceted fusion of music that was uniquely distinct from the other competing musical forms. The singers who produced this brand-new wave of regional music were for the most part teenagers who were still under the authority of their parents. Most of them were not in college, and they came from working-class families. The high schools that produced these artists were inner city schools in New York, New Jersey, and Pennsylvania. They generally ranked from the lower middle to upper middle of their class, with some exceptions. They came from urban communities in the height of social unrest, changing values, and shifting traditions. Many of these students were first- and second-generation immigrants whose parents or grandparents came from the old country. They all looked to family as a cohesive force, as well as to their church or synagogue. The clear majority were non-African-Americans who were visionaries, and who believed that they could make it in the music world if they gave it a strong shot. These teens believed that they had nothing to lose and everything to gain in the pursuit of something they loved. Their musical style was unlike any other musical genre style or sound ever produced. This sound can be traced to the first wave of African-Americans coming to the eastern seaboard after the first World War. What happened afterwards left an urban signature along the Hudson River tributary cities of New Jersey, New York, and Pennsylvania. Moreover, its mark spread along the eastern seaboard of major urban cities. The new urban sound was called *Hudson*.

The Hudson Sound is acappella vocal group singing in the R&B fashion, a distinctive style that was born on the banks of the Hudson River where New York and New Jersey meet. It is an extraordinary singing style and class that is represented by seven basic features. These seven distinct markings or components make the Hudson Sound unique. Let us examine this new regional sound, and decipher what makes this sound different from other musical sounds such as Motown, Folk, and Country. Let us travel back in time to unravel why the great majority of major record companies, historians, and pundits rejected, or at least failed to give credit to, a regional sound that was both indigenous and urban folk in nature. Over fifty years have passed, and we still see a reluctance to acknowledge vocal group singing in the R&B, Street Corner, or Doo-Wop singing style as a sustainable sound.[4]

Thousands of people all over the world have embraced this sound, and it is still growing. Let's examine the unique aspects of the Hudson Sound.

---

4 Author Note: Preference is given to R&B and Street Corner Singing over Doo-Wop. See Abraham J. Santiago, *Acappella Living in the Shadows 1963-1973: A Social History* (Harbinger Press, 2016) pg. 27.

PART TWO

THE WAY IT WAS

CHAPTER TWO

THE EMERGENCE OF A NEW SOUND

First, it is important that we define this new sound. Acappella is an Italian word that means in the style of the chapel. It is usually identified as choral or ensemble singing without musical instrumentation in a sacred or religious setting. It is important to note that acappella originated within the cultural context of the Christian faith. Today, the term has a more generic meaning than the original definition. Most colleges and universities, both small and large, have some sort of acappella chorale. Music organizations, associations, and clubs have acappella singers. With that said, we need to re-define what the term meant over fifty years ago in the urban inner cities of America. Over fifty years ago, when first coined by acappella pioneer Irving "Slim" Rose, owner of Times Square Records, the term meant vocal group harmonization in the rhythm and blues style. It did not mean anything else. It was Rose who changed the spelling from *a cappella* to *acappella* to give the term clarity and distinctness.[5] Keep in mind that the origin of rhythm and blues style has at its root the religious Christian context of the Afro-American experience. In actuality, the style's Christian religious roots go back to the renaissance period. Lawrence Pitilli, Associate Professor at St. John's University, notes the following:

Doo-wop acappella has its ancestral roots in the fifteenth-century religious music, and reinvents itself over a course of five-century timeline.[6]

Fifteenth century music, which was largely Christian, influenced acappella vocal group singing, and influenced the African American

---

[5] The author uses the word spelled *acappella* throughout this book instead of *a cappella*.

[6] Lawrence Pitilli, *Doo Wop Acappella: A Story of Street Corners, Echoes, and Three-Part Harmonies* (Rowman & Littlefield, 2016), pg. 2.

experience. By way of example, the late Ray Charles turned his first big hit, "*I Got a Woman*," from the hit song "It *Must be Jesus*" by the Southern Tones. Charles made the song a hit by changing the lyrics and keeping the melody. The colored community did not accept what it deemed "the devil's music," as it was a desecration of the Gospel of Jesus Christ; but with time, the style was accepted within their social structure.[7] Since acappella singing is performed without a band or orchestra, the focus is always on the singers. The concentration is always on the singers' blending of voices or harmonizing. Generally speaking, singers had a lead, first and second tenor, baritone and a base.

---

[7] https://www.udiscovermusic.com/in-depth-features/gospel-influenced-rhythm-n-blues/

Wayne Stierle, Gus Gorsset, and Stan Krause
(Courtesy Stierle Archives)

#1

First, singing was done acappella, in an aural harmonic fashion. Singers absorbed songs by listening to a commercial recording or a vocal group. They had no sheet music to read, and learned their parts in a natural auditory fashion. If a singer was off key, even slightly, it was immediately pointed out. Keep in mind that the vast majority of these singers had no formal training in music. They memorized their parts by familiarization of the songs and repeated repetition.

The acappella singers literally learned their skills on urban street corners, boys' bathrooms, subway stations, and hallways. As well as imitating the doo-wop hits of the day found on their 45-rpm records.[8]

When harmonizing, they put their "ears to the grooves" and learned their individual parts. Singers then did not use vocal gymnastics such as beat boxing, vocal chopping, or other vocal maneuvers to create a sound that resembles an instrument, as we have today. Groups sang as naturally as they could. The simple triads and basic harmonic chords of this music made the Hudson Sound unique.

…Five young men stood around a tape recorder in a church cellar and sang. They couldn't afford a band but wouldn't have bothered with one if things had been different. They always practiced without music; doing so simply ensured perfect harmony.[9]

When groups sang live, they used no devices to recall their notes. They entered the stage to sing on key. The acappella pioneers introduced a new commercial venture in the music recording business. Prior to the birth of acappella in 1963 as a new pop genre, there was no commercial industry that recorded singers who sang strictly acappella. For the first time in American music history, independent record com-

---

8 Ibid pg.117
9 The Rise And Fall Of Acappella -Bill Millar: *Record Mirror*, 4 June 1972

panies were founded specifically to record acappella artists. This had never before been undertaken in music history. An acappella industry emerged and became a niche within the corporate music sphere. Acappella infiltrated the shadowy business of music, and major record labels were not interested in the genre. Bear in mind that the birth of this new industry was not planned, its success was completely fortuitous. It is important to note that during World War II, Decca Records produced acappella recordings for a group called the Song Spinners in support of the war effort. The end result was that their song *"Comin In on a Wing and a Prayer"* reached #12 on the charts in 1943, and became the first acappella recording on the Billboard charts. The same song was sung by the Golden Gate Quartet on the Okeh label as a gospel song. Major record companies such as Atlantic, Mercury, Victor, and others viewed acappella as an anomaly—an unprofitable business venture not worthy of consideration. Fileti writes:

"If industry pro like Atlantic's Jerry Wexler subtly mocked the "Golden Age of Acappella" (his words), it was because of the off-key and poorly recorded singles, which appealed to many young group harmony fans in the early sixties." [10]

It was considered then, and now to a lesser degree, an albatross within the music industry. The concept of producing and recording singers without a band or orchestra was out-of-the-box thinking. For the pioneers who started this new genre, the business enterprise proved to be mildly profitable. The current mantra at that time among acappella record producers was that they were not making money. This was their chant, because many groups wanted remunerations or stipends for the shows they played and for the sale of their records. However, this lack of funds was a ruse to keep groups from complaining about their failure to be paid. Today, some of these early music makers still have unreleased master tapes collecting dust. A case in point, is acappella pioneer Bobby Miller founder of Old Timer Records. His unreleased recordings of the 1966 acappella show at the RKO Fordham Theatre in the Bronx is an example. Those recordings of Miller were finally released in 2010 on a CD- *"I Dug Acappella"*. It included twenty-three

---

10 http//lulusko.www7.50megs.com/timessquare/tsr.htm

tracks and 5 unreleased recordings. The following groups on those unreleased songs were the 5 Sharks, Shadows, Notations, Royal Counts, and Concepts. Regrettably, those who sang decades ago would like to have any and all recordings released for posterity.[11] Finally, in the end, major record labels missed out on what could have been a gold mine of talent and money if only they had summoned the courage to think outside the box. Going back to what was said previously, the real losers in this new, untapped undertaking were the major record companies. These companies refused and failed to hear the voices of neighborhood young people and to respond to a new sound. In a sense, record executives were the condescending swamp creatures of the music industry. Their long-established monopoly in music made record executives the established authority on what worked and what didn't. There was always an askance towards acappella. From their perspective, acappella was considered "low art" or degenerate art (*entartete kunst* as the Nazis would say). Not only that, but they had no fear that acappella would ever become a powerful influence like Hip Hop or what Rap is today, even though they are filled with destructive messages and vulgarity.[12] For executives, acappella did not work, and therefore it was not worth investing in music that would not pay dividends in the future. These executives totally lacked objectivity; for those in the industry, acappella was flawed, and its singers were not the *crème de la crème*. In the very beginning, homemade recordings were generally a sham with poor quality work. Many of the early recordings were made in basements, closets, or bathrooms. Some recordings were released with group members talking in the background. Their early recording equipment usually consisted of one or two tracks. Wayne Stierle said the following:

"Recording the first acapella groups was a rough and tumble experience because almost anyone who can sing on the corner, or in the hallway, is somewhat stunned by their first meeting with a microphone in a studio. Part of the process is getting a group to loosen up, and not all groups could do that."[13]

---

11 https://www.discogs.com/artist/303086-Bobby-Miller
12 https://www.udiscovermusic.com/stories/politics-of-hip-hop/.
13 Email: March 3, 2019

Lastly, acappella was a medium that no one could dance to. All this, added to the uniqueness of acappella, and made it more attractive to young people. In a real sense, record executives were intolerant of new ideas outside their sphere of influence. In addition, record companies had tremendous power and influence over their singers.

Moreover, record labels were involved in what some would call cultural hegemony. Cultural hegemony in the music industry was powerful, and labels exerted their authority on the powerless and took advantage of them. This is clearly seen today in Hip Hop music.[14] In addition, this can be seen in R&B stars like R. Kelly.[15] They all repeated the same mantra—that acappella groups were upstart novices. In a sense, they were expressing a tautology. Astonishingly, rarely did an A&R executive hear group members sing a live song. In some cases, they may have heard acappella music on the radio. Some would hire a self-styled A&R man like the popular and skilled vocalist Richard Barrett, who knew what was going on, and who knew the pulse of the neighborhood.[16]

The major record companies could have easily communicated with music makers like Rose, Stierle, Krause, and others, and say, "bring a few groups to my studio so that I can hear how they sound." Record producers could have made a deal with these young entrepreneurs and make something happen, but they didn't. You can rest assured that if that had happened, these groups would have been polished to the till, and something might have come out of it. Moreover, the labels were not interested in investing in groups musically and helping them to achieve the harmonic sound they would have wanted to achieve in a recording. Record companies were following a new cultural pop

---

14 https://itsactuallyimportant.wordpress.com/2014/04/18/cultural-hegemony-in-the-music-industry/.
15 https://www.nytimes.com/2019/01/04/arts/music/surviving-r-kelly.html
16 https://itunes.apple.com/ca/album/the-valentines-meet-the-van-dykes-doo-wop/562249269.

trend, and for them, group R&B singing was not it. Bands were in, not vocal groups singing in the R&B style of the 1950s. They wanted something trendy. In all fairness, the record labels were partially correct. However, they overlooked an important factor—young people with the spending power to purchase records. Ultimately, young adults were the powerbrokers who made a band, a singer, or a group a success, not the record company. They could make a record a hit or a failure. It should be noted that major record companies had a lot of money to promote, advertise, and market their vocalists and songs. Yet in all this, the record companies weren't willing to invest in groups in general, just like in the decade before them.

For this reason, executives of the major record companies viewed the acappella phenomena as a waste of time and money. They did not fit the mold of compliance to social conceptions of the music industry. They were a fad and novelty; nothing more. What they wanted were young vocalists who could sing instantaneously without investing in them. It's no wonder that many great vocal groups of the 1950s closed shop. In addition, groups in the 1950s realized that they were the recipients of theft, fraud and not getting royalty checks. Also, age was a factor and executives considered them too old to record in the 1960s. The record companies of the 1950s deserted them. Some have blamed the invasion of the British bands as part of the reason for the downturn of group singing. For this reason, some have said that the R&B vocal group singing or doo-wop era died out when the 1960s came along. Journalist Bill Millar holds to this classic myth about R&B group singing. Millar a respected journalist and a knowledgeable music historian failed to understand the social-cultural context of the times. It never died.

The English invasion halted white doo-wop overnight. Apart from the occasional throwback (for example, the Casinos who scored with 'Then You Can Tell Me Goodbye' in 1967), the style was simply wiped out of existence." [17]

---

[17] http://teachrock.org/article/doo-wop-at-the-hop/

The scarcity of commercial recording of 1950s groups during the 1960s and 70s was made up by a new breed of vocal group singers, who sang a mélange of soul, classic rhythm and blues, and pop songs recording them without a band or orchestra. B. Lee Cooper says, that doo-wop began within a 15-year time period 1948-1963.[18] His timeline corresponds to the birth of acappella in 1963 as a new pop genre.

For the majors, making money was a priority, not reinvesting in groups or remolding their group persona. There were not many 50s groups who reinvented themselves during the 1960s and beyond. Little Anthony and the Imperials did, and so did Johnny Maestro. Maestro former lead singer of The Crests connected with the Brooklyn Bridge. Yet in all this, mistreatment and not helping groups succeeded on its own was par for the course. A classic example is the poor treatment of Motown girl trio the Andantes.

The trio sang background on more than 20,000 Motown songs, upward of 90 percent of the company's output before its 1972 move to Los Angeles... Yet most Motown fans still don't know the Andantes' story.[19]

According to David Goldblatt, Millar, estimated that during the 1950s there was roughly 15,000 black vocal groups that recorded during that time period. If that was the case, how was it possible for the whole music genre consisting of both black and white groups disappear or be wiped out of existence? [20] The music business was a cut-throat business that dissected, chopped, diced, and did not give credit to whom credit was due. By way of example, Motown executives would emphasize to their employees, we are all family, but in reality, many singers were abused and not treated fairly as "family members". Moreover, the record indus-

---

18 B. Lee Cooper (2014) Doo Wop: The R&B Vocal Group Sound, 1950–1960, by Various Artists; Doo Wop: The Rock & Roll Vocal Group Sound, 1957–1961, by Various Artists, Popular Music and Society, 37:4, 513-516, DOI: 10.1080/03007766.2013.835918

19 https://www.aarp.org/entertainment/music/info-2018/motown-girl-group-the-andantes.html

20 https://onlinelibrary.wiley.com/doi/abs/10.1111/j.1540-6245.2012.01546.x

try as a whole, with some exceptions, was a culture of mendacity and scheming. The owners of acappella record labels were viewed by the major record companies as provocateurs and rebels. The truth of the matter is that these young men (who were all under twenty-five) were visionaries who knew the business, and who had the determination to make something happen. These music makers were street smart, and they knew where groups lived and performed. Where would an A&R man from the suburbs of a major record company hear a group sing? How would he know whether the neighborhoods where these groups lived and sang were safe to visit? These Vinyl City music makers knew these group members personally, knew where they lived, and knew where they hung out and sang. Although the music makers may have lacked a university education and sophistication, they had the advantage of being street-smart in a time when the cultural ethos was changing. These young men, who were girded with determination, tenacity, and ambition, started their own record labels to the amazement of the major record companies. They had the audacity to do something that was never been done before, and they did it. In a real sense, they gave the major record companies the proverbial finger.

In the end, they were the winners—not the major record labels. This included record companies who were on top of their form, like Atlantic Records, Motown Records, and Stax Records. These labels all failed to seize the moment. It would not have been difficult for the major record labels to form a subsidiary acappella label. How complicated would it have been for Motown to record the Supremes acappella, or for Philadelphia International Records to record Harold Melvin & the Blue Notes? These major records companies would have saved money on musicians' studio work and live tours. Again, this failure shows their lack of vision, business shrewdness, and understanding of what young people wanted. How problematic would it have been to lease, hire, or buy out these music makers' record labels? These are questions that have not been explored at all. That is why individuals such as Wayne Stierle, the late Stan Krause, and others have always maintained the absurdity of major record labels not investing in and recording groups singing acappella. Fortunately, decades later, acappella appeared again in the new millennium with the very first TV show about acappella, *The Sing Off*. For the first time since WWII, a major record company, Sony Records, realized how engaging and powerful acappella can be. The winner of the Sing Off, Nota, received a hundred-thousand-dollar recording contract with Sony. Moreover, Nota was honored to sing with the legendary vocalist Smokey Robinson at the end of the show.[21] In the end, the music makers of the 1960s were vindicated, acappella is worth investing in. Sadly, even though progresses were made in all this, acappella street corner singing as a genre is still not recognized within the R&B music category. It recognizes Funk, Soul, Rap but not acappella.[22] Lastly, the first and only person who recorded a group from the 1950s acappella (LP) recording was Wayne Stierle with the Shells.

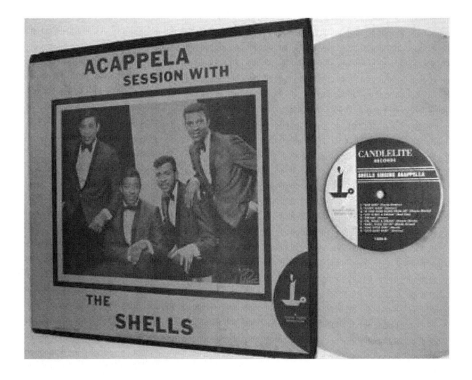

---

21 https://www.youtube.com/watch?v=L_l-kLF72
22 Cahoon, Brad. "Rhythm and Blues Music: Overview." New Georgia Encyclopedia. 11 December 2014.

#2

Second, the Hudson Sound was a meeting of the twains. It was a fusion of two assemblages of vocal bravura from two different communities on both sides of the Hudson River—New York, and New Jersey. The two communities were rivals in a healthy and competitive way to demonstrate their superiority in song arrangement and harmony. It was a fusion of two distinct sounds coming from the five boroughs of New York City, Jersey City across the river, and its neighboring communities. The coming together of two communities from both sides of the Hudson River along the acappella corridor that stretched from Boston to the Philadelphia-Pittsburg area became a distinctive regional sound. A case in point is the cocky bragging among the Royal Counts from Jersey City when they heard that a group from Brooklyn would sing at their next show. All the teasing and put downs, all in fun, made it clear that no New York group would ever overshadow a Jersey group. Jersey pride was paramount, and any group from the other side *best not mess with us!*

Fortunately, the Brooklyn group was the Persuasions, featuring lead singer Jerry Lawson, who became the unofficial ambassador of the Hudson Sound. The Persuasions brought acappella across America, and ignited people both young and old. Finally, acappella had become the social glue that cemented cities and neighborhoods together. It was the unforgettable intros, the magical harmonies, the special songs, and the soaring vocals that made the sound distinctive. There was an urban musical syncretism that provided unity among a diverse community of singers and ethnic backgrounds. Both localities developed their own vocal style and linguistic flair that meshed into a new sound. It was not intentional, but led to a process of assimilation of cultures, and the production of something unique. In the end, both sides of the Hudson delivered their own arrangements and presentation of songs that brought audiences applauding and cheering for more. Both sides brought synergy and drew hundreds to live overflowing shows. In a sense, they were the urban Beatles of the local neighborhoods and barrios. It is also important to remember, that the Hudson Sound as a regional genre sound was a powerful force on the Atlantic Coast. Groups from the West Coast could not come close to the emotional and artistic harmonies of groups from the northern cities of the Atlantic. Vocal groups in general from the 1950s, and beyond had a reputation as being the best of the best. Groups from the West or Mid-West could not compete with groups from the Northeast musically. Millar said the following about groups from the East Coast, and then cites Johnny Otis perspective on West Coast groups:

"There was a depth to the East Coast vocal group tradition that the rest of the country lacked... Johnny Otis remarked: 'On the East, they have such nice harmonies, musically, artistically ... but dear friends like the Penguins, the Medallions and those other West Coast groups were horrible. I used to talk to my bassman and my trumpet player and we used to say, "There must be something here in the water that causes that".[23]

So, in the end, acappella groups inherited their artistic-musical style from 1950s groups. It is no wonder that the Hudson Sound has its roots on the East Coast, and more specifically, the Hudson River metropolitan area.

---

23 http://teachrock.org/article/doo-wop-at-the-hop/

BIG PARTY TONIGHT
TUESDAY
DECEMBER 20th
CAKE - GIVEAWAYS - DRINK SPECIALS
INCREDIBLE MUSIC & DANCING
PARTY TIME 7-11 PM
COVER $6 - 18+

CELEBRATING THE MUSIC OF JOHNNY OTIS

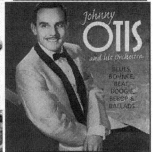

CLUB VICENTE
IN THE BEAUTIFUL DON VICENTE HISTORIC INN AT 14TH ST AND 9TH AVE
ACROSS THE STREET FROM HILLSBOROUGH COMMUNITY COLLEGE YBOR CAMPUS

THE PENGUINS

Dream Tones
(Courtesy Shively Archives)

Jersey City Skyline

New York City Skyline
(Courtesy Samuel Gottscho Archive

#3

Third, the Hudson Sound was a tenor sound as opposed to the soulful-indigo style of music that emerged from places like Memphis, Detroit, and Muscle Shoals. When we compare the Hudson Sound to the unwavering soulful sound coming from Motown or other regions like Muscle Shoals, Alabama, where Wilson Picket flourished, we get a sense of how unique the sound was. The sound was unique not only because it was acappella, but because of how the sound was achieved. There was always a constant rearrangement and experimentation of songs and harmonies.[24] The Hudson Sound is reminiscent of the style of music that existed during the 1920s, 30s, and 40s, when tenor singers dominated the theatrical and musical venues of that period. Then, the scene changed with the appearance of a singer by the name of Bing Crosby, who changed the landscape of pop singing by introducing a mellow, rich baritone sound to the public arena. His voice influenced the public perception that baritones had a place in the musical field alongside tenors. Friedwald comments:

(Courtesy Crosby archives)

---

24 https://theaudiophileman.com/vocal-harmonies/

Crosby is the biggest influence on American popular singing. Before Bing there was no baritone in the popular field only tenors. Crosby made America baritone-conscious and popularized the rich deep tones that move people so much. Crosby revolutionized modern singing. Crosby achieved all this largely from his own absorption of black style and served a function of such importance to the development of Afro-American vocal music partly because he returned to blacks what was rightfully theirs.[25]

The acappella era re-introduced, in historically cyclical fashion, the tenor vocal range of singing. Not all who sang acappella during this period had sky-high harmonies or prominent tenors leads. However, a sweeping general view of the many entertainers represented during this time would conclude that a sizable percentage of such groups featured tenors. This would not be what we call today a mellow baritone or soulful singing scale. Now, there are exceptions, but by and large, the Hudson Sound featured a tenor scale. For example, groups such as The Persuasions would be considered to have a "soulful" baritone range. Vocal groups such as The Royal Counts, Notations, and The Chessmen are examples of soulful singers. These groups could reach the tenor scale effortlessly.

By way of illustration, The Royal Counts produced an LP album entitled "Acappella Soul" in the mid-1960s that had all the features of falsetto, and a gritty, soulful sound. However, as we review acappella groups of the 1960s, we should note that they represented the finest of non-African-American singing groups who did not pretend to be soulful. They sang their own interpretations of material in their own way. Their musical repertoire included everything from current hits of the time to Broadway tunes. In a sense, they fit what we might call an eclectic or champagne style. The Persuasions would fit into this category. However, Jerry Lawson, like the late Ray Charles, never wanted

---

[25] Friedwald, W. *Jazz Singing: America's Great Voices From Bessie Smith To Bebop And Beyond* (New York: Da Capo Press, 1990), pg.252.

the public or the music industry to attach him to a certain musical style.[26] Charles said the following:

I don't call myself a blues singer or a jazz singer or a country singer or whatever. I just call myself a singer that sings the blues, a singer that can sing jazz, a singer that knows how to sing country music in my own way. [27]

Examples of prominent vocal groups that exercised tenor ranges are Del Capris, Five Jades, Autumns, Savoys, and Heartaches. It is important to understand that the tenor scale of singing among acappella vocal groups resurfaced unexpectedly in the 1960s. The influence of some groups from the 1950s, such as Little Anthony and the Imperials, Frankie Lymon and the Teenagers, and groups like the Jive Five, may have had a subliminal impact on urban teenagers and similar groups. These urban teenagers, mostly non-African-Americans, sang these songs knowing that they did not have the mellow, low range-gritty soulful style that was shaping American music within rhythm and blues. When Soul came on the scene in the early 1960s, the genre changed, and awakened the public to a new sound. It is interesting that the Hudson Sound was competing with Soul as well as many other musical art forms. They were competing in the shadows, below the radar, and they were drawing massive crowds.

---

26 https://www.youtube.com/watch?v=NSPbeOiEO3Q.
27 Mike Evans, *Ray Charles, The Birth of Soul* (Omnibus Press, 2005), p. 115.

ACAPPELLA SHOW

THE CHESSMEN
THE ROYAL COUNTS
THE DEL CAPRIS - THE VALIDS
JO-ANNE AND THE HEARTACHES
THE ALPACAS - M.C. RON LUCIANO
AND MANY SURPRISE GROUPS

ACAPPELLA A GO-GO-GIRLS

FOX THEATER 309 Main Street
Hackensack, N.J.

Tuesday Nite, August 30th

Show Starts 8:30

Everybody Welcome : Donation, $2.00

TICKETS AVAILABLE AT: FOX BOX OFFICE
RELIC RACK: 136 Main Street, Hackensack, N. J.
JOURNAL SQUARE RECORD CENTER, 2856 Kennedy Blvd., Jersey City, N. J.
TIMES SQUARE RECORDS, New York or send $2.00 for each ticket to:
RON LUCIANO, 37 Woodside Avenue, Hasbrouck Heights, N. J.

A RON LUCIANO PRODUCTION

(Courtesy Calamito Archives Circa 1967)

The Royal Counts

Stan Krause, Acappella Pioneer
(Courtesy Krause Archives)

#4

Fourthly, singing groups mostly consisted of non-African-Americans who were nurtured on rhythm and blues.[28] The singers were predominantly brothers of another shade who were hip to the music that was being played on the radio and who were totally acquainted with musical groups of the past. Millar says the following about non-African groups or white groups:

White doo-wop's best exponents sprang from lower status minorities. By WASP standards, 'white' is really a misnomer since it was the Italian, Hispanic and Polish kids who took to the subways in search of the perfect echo. Many of the Puerto Ricans, next to the blacks the lowest on the social scale, were recruited from street gangs and black/Puerto Rican combinations, like Frankie Lymon and the Teenagers, were not uncommon.[29]

Vocal adaptations and vocal alterations by ethnic groups such as Italians, Irish, Jews, and Puerto Ricans maintained the heritage of the three- and four-part harmonies of the rhythm and blues style. These young singers were raised and reared on rhythm and blues. Their mentors were groups such as The Harptones, Ravens, Swallows, Crests, Five Keys, and many more. Young teenagers attended live shows at the Brooklyn Paramount, Apollo Theatre, and in New Jersey. Teenagers listened to disc jockey radio personalities like Alan Freed, Jocko, Cousin Brucie, Jerry Blavat, and Murray the K, to name a few. In real life, these singers were immersed in the black music sounds of vocal groups. For them, there was an element of cultural appropriation and adaptation within the confines of interpreting specific songs. However, they were not what we would call today afro-centric in presentation. They sang in their own way, and did not pretend to be something that

---

28 Abraham J. Santiago, *Acappella Living in the Shadows 1963-1973: A Social History* (Harbinger Press, 2016), p. 57.
29 read: http://teachrock.org/article/doo-wop-at-the-hop/

they were not. They sang their songs with a strong element of clarity and passion.

The Connotations
(Courtesy Katz Archives)

#5

Fifthly, the acappella movement was a male-dominated assortment of vocal groups with almost no female members. It was truly a male-dominated genre in which testosterone flowed like musical chords. Female acappella vocal groups were scarce, and these groups did not venture out to sing on street corners or to seek that elusive echo that so many male groups sought, even though girl groups widely commanded respect on the airwaves. Indeed, the genre was an insular-minded assembly of young men who believed that girls belonged at home or in school, not in the street hanging out and trying to hit a few tunes. It was considered culturally and socially unacceptable for young men to observe a group of girls singing on a street corner. To put it in today's vernacular, this was a guy's thing, and it was not cool when girls encroached. This was the prevailing norm during this period in a culture that was changing rapidly. It is important to understand, however, that many "girl groups" of the 1960s were powerhouses, and many of them came from Motown. Sadly, many great female groups that sang acappella were not allowed to experience the possibility of stardom simply because of family constraints. The Emeralds, for example, were an incredible group with Candice Crawford as lead singer, yet Crawford never made an acappella recording with her group. She recorded a few songs on the Catamount label with the Royal Counts, and her vocal lead is extraordinary.[30] Even though there were many girl groups to emulate, none sang acappella. The period saw a shortage of girl groups singing acappella. Sadly, even today, it is difficult to find female groups that sing doo-wop acappella.

---

30 https://www.youtube.com/watch?v=LYK-oF2idBc

Candice Crawford
(Courtesy Santiago Archives)

#6

Sixth, the Hudson Sound was a group performance act of quintets and quartets. There were no solo acts in which individuals sang acappella on stage or made solo acappella recordings. There were no duets or trios.[31] The groups were generally all-male quintets and quartets. When groups performed on stage, their dance routines were simple, reflecting the songs they sang. They were well-groomed and wore suits or matching outfits, and always looked their best. Bob Waters, a member of the Five Fashions, has noted that these groups dressed their best before going on stage.[32] It was in this historical and social context that the Hudson Sound stood out among the other regional musical sounds of the 1960s. Keep in mind that this period saw the birth of the "dressing down" of vocal bands and individual singers. In many cases, vocal bands were not well-groomed, and their outfits did not match. They wore the clothes that they wanted to wear to make a statement to the public, and to provide cultural oxygen to their fan base. There are exceptions; however, almost all the R&B and Soul vocal groups of this period were dressed immaculately, and so were the individual singers of the period.

The Five Sharks
(Courtesy Bank Archives)

---

31 https://www.youtube.com/watch?v=jC90lHWnX70.
32 *Street Corner Harmony* -Documentary Film (Mellow Sound Productions, 2010).

#7

Seventh, the Hudson Sound was never owned by a record label such as Motown Records, Philadelphia International Records, or Stax Records, which would have promoted their specific sounds. No record label claimed the Hudson Sound as its own. The Hudson Sound operated independently as a nonconformist genre, as new record companies emerged and challenged established record companies. As time progressed, better-trained studio engineers evolved, bringing new equipment, and better-polished singing groups emerged. This is not to say that there were not skillful singers and engineers during this time. As one hears the recordings of groups years later, and revisits their live shows, the very same groups that sang decades before during the 60s were still singing in the 1980s, 1990s, and into the new millennium. The argument that all groups who sang during the first wave (1963–1973) of group revival were amateurish is utterly and demonstrably false.[33]

The Five Fashions

---

33 Abraham J. Santiago, *The Untold Story United Group Harmony Association* (Mellow Sound Press, 2014), pg.61.

The Persuasions, Ambassadors of the Hudson Sound
(Courtesy Lawson Archives)

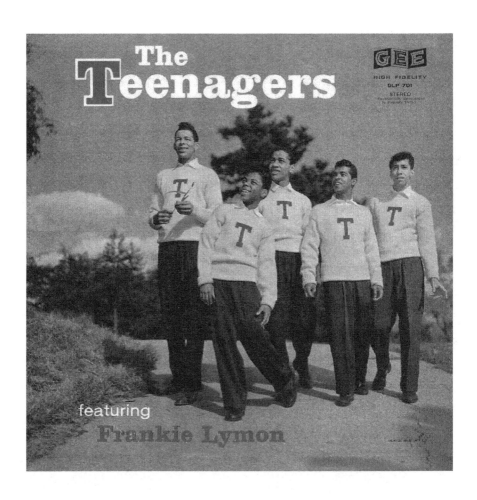

DINO & THE HEARTSPINNERS
(Courtesy G. Scott Archives)

PART THREE

SOCIAL BOUNDARIES

CHAPTER THREE

HIGH SCHOOL DAYS

Being a young adult in the 1960s was a thrill, because it was then that we discovered who we were. Some discovered who they really were in college, at work, or in the military. High school was a place to connect with friends, make new friends, engage in sports and clubs, go on field trips, and engage in a host of other activities. It was a place to find your dream girl or guy. High school was the place to be, for it was a social outlet for all teens, much like a church or synagogue. It was a place to show off your athletic and physical adeptness to the opposite sex. But most of all, it was a place to prepare to be a future bride or groom, and to discover your vocation. With that said, teens during this period of social unrest were living through a changing worldview. Teens were in the crosshairs of a changing cultural ethos in which moral absolutes were challenged. Teens often believed in God, family, and country. The views that they held as children, however, were being challenged by those who said that there were no moral absolutes, and that all views were relative. It is safe to say that teens lived in their own world, a city made of vinyl that was strictly theirs.

Those who believed and promoted the dogma that there were no absolutes fractured our cultural well-being. Believing in something outside of ourselves, and having a point of reference, kept us from being entangled with the abuse of our neighborhoods. In a sense, belief was an anchor. We learned from our family respect, responsibility, and resourcefulness. That was often challenged by the use of drugs, open sex, contempt towards authority, and a host of other things. Fortunately, our high school teachers were there to help us and to point us in the right direction. These teachers didn't deviate from what we were taught from home—rather, they upheld our family values and encouraged us to be the best that we could be. Our teachers and staff, from the school principal to the janitor, encouraged us to pursue the values that we were taught at home.

Furthermore, most high schools along the Hudson River Metropolitian Area in New York and New Jersey were culturally and socially innocuous, although some were underprivileged. Yes, there were street gangs, ethnic and racial rivalry, and drugs. If a fight errupted among young people, generally it was the "fist" that prevailed. In spite of this, there was always a sense that help was avaiable, and that there were places and people from which we could receive the encouragement and direction we needed to move ahead. What schools lacked in terms of equipment, books, and teaching staff was compensated by the outlet for students to engage in music. Music cemented many students in solidarity. For those who engaged in music, the scholastic experience was different from sports, which was a seasonal practice. Music is an all-year event. It was for this reason that students became involved in music to stay focused and out of trouble. Music lured us out of trouble, and perhaps led us into our vocation.

Schools in New York City, Philadelphia, and Jersey City produced outstanding musicians, songwriters, singers, and a host of other celebrities. Carole King, for example, graduated from James Madison High School in Brooklyn, which in a way reinforced and solidified her musical experience. In the city of Philadelphia, Patti La Belle attended John Bartram High School, where she began her career as a singer by entering a talent contest and winning, which later led her to start a vocal group, and eventually led her to stardom. In Jersey City, there was Kool and the Gang, who attended Lincoln High School. Their band would go on to sell millions of records worldwide. These artists sharpened their skills in high school, and the outcome was musical success.

PART FOUR

HIGH SCHOOL ROMANCE

CHAPTER FOUR

THE FERRISSIAN CONNECTION

Every high school across America has produced someone who made it to the top of his or her class. Some schools have produced students who went on to study at prestigious universities like Princeton University, Juilliard School of Music, and California State University. Many schools specialize in music, art, science, math, business, and a host of other disciplines. Some schools are privileged to have exceptional students who are inclined towards a certain discipline, or who have a certain gift or talent. This is true in life, and it continues to be that way. One remarkable school seems to have a propensity for vocal-music talent, and that school is located in Jersey City, New Jersey. Over fifty years ago, this unique school produced many students who attended high-ranking universities, produced men and women who went into politics, academia, and served in the military as officers, and saw several students found successful businesses. It was a public urban school that struggled to provide the best it could for its students, who came from a cross-section of humanity. The community in which it was located was changing due to the cultural upheaval that took place in this period.

Yet despite these changes, this high school stood out. This high school managed, in the face of the turmoil of the 1960s, to set itself apart, and to produce an array of talented individuals in many fields. For some reason, this high school became the major center for vocal groups singing in the R&B style. At the time, the school was located on Cole Street, and the school is James J. Ferris High School. In a short period during the 1960s, it produced many great singing groups. Their inspiration and encouragement did not come primarily from entertainers, but rather from two great music teachers. Mrs. Helen Marrow, the school's Choir Director, and Mr. Mortimer Epstein, the Band Director, greatly inspired these students. These two individuals created a climate in which students were taught that anyone can do anything if they put their minds to it.

It's no wonder that Ferrissians became opera singers, symphony musicians, and songwriters—the credit belongs to their teachers and their high school environment. Even today, many of those who once attended Ferris High School continue to participate in music in some fashion. Ferris High School became one of the few schools that have managed to survive against all obstacles, and continues to do so today. It is well-known fact that during school hours, as students transitioned from one class to another, an eruption would often take place. Occasionally, the sound of students talking and laughing would be interrupted by the sound of voices emerging from the marble bathrooms to the hallways. The student monitors, who were tasked with ensuring that no one loitered in the hallways after the bell rang, would find a few students who made it without a pass when the bell rang. Suddenly, out of nowhere, a harmonic blend of voices would seep from under the bathroom doors into the hallways. The students in class would hear the songs that were sung, and they would begin swaying back and forth to the song instead of paying attention to the teacher. This major interruption caused many teachers to leave the classroom and rebuke the group for disturbing the class. The moment that the teacher left, the chatter and laughter began. It was all part of adolescent behavior and a public-school environment in which music and vinyl reigned.

Ferris High School was no different from any other public school in Jersey City or across the Hudson. There were certain crowds of teens that admired, loved, and followed various groups, and that supported these groups in their endeavor to become great entertainers. These teens were what we would now call "groupies." In a sense, these singing groups were celebrities among their own peers.

There were often battles between the groups—not a physical fight, but a vocal battle. The competition was tough and full of ego and name calling—some in fun, and some not in fun. Groups wanted to be the best of the best, even if it meant stealing song arrangements, recruiting members from other groups, and pocketing original songs. Groups wanted a sound of their own that would be unique from the others. There was always competition, as groups sought a competitive edge over others. Many times, it was a group's choice of songs, song arrangement, tight harmony, lead singer, and the way they dressed that put them over the top. These assets often determined the success of the group.

Group success was also heightened by humility. It was always best not to brag, because this was a great turn off. Having a beautiful girl on your arm was the ultimate success. Having the best-looking girl in the school was a stamp of approval among group members. Some girls wanted to be in the limelight, and dating a group member gave them bragging rights. These elements made the group singing ethos a time of fun, romance, and friendship. There are no quantitative data to measure which high schools in Jersey City during the 1960s and 70s produced the most vocal groups. However, it appears from the evidence of public high school yearbooks and local neighborhood gatherings, that Ferris may have produced the most. If that is true, then Ferris is truly a remarkable high school.

MRS. HELEN MARROW, CHOIR DIRECTOR
(Courtesy Santiago Archives)

MR. MORTIMER EPSTEIN, BAND DIRECTOR
(Courtesy Santiago Archives)

James J. Ferris High School
(Courtesy Santiago Archives)

ABRAHAM J. SANTIAGO

VOCAL GROUPS MEMBERS FROM FERRIS HIGH SCHOOL

The Corals
(Courtesy Santiago Archives)

The Heartaches

The Medallions
(Courtesy Santiago Archives)

The Concepts
(Courtesy Santiago Archives)

The Emeralds
(Courtesy Santiago Archives)

The Valentines
(Courtesy Santiago Archives)

The Latin Kings
(Courtesy Santiago Archives)

The Del Capris

THE UNIQUES
(Courtesy Calamito archives)

The Emeralds and The Concepts
(Courtesy Santiago Archives)

2 Smooth
(Courtesy Amorosa Archives)

Neighborhood Wish
(Courtesy Dalessandro Archives)

Ferris High School Year Book Cover

ABRAHAM J. SANTIAGO

REUNION TIME
CLASS OF 1963 TO 1969

(Courtesy Santiago Archives)

ABE SANTIAGO AND JUAN PEREZ
(Courtesy Santiago Archives)

PART FIVE

OUR VINYL RECORDS

CHAPTER FIVE

PIONEER ACAPPELLA RECORD LABELS

When Irving "Slim" Rose, the founder and pioneer of acappella, began recording vocal groups and releasing acappella recordings commercially, it immediately became a sensation. It was a time when young people were seeking something different. The "British Invasion" of the early- to mid-1960s had a widespread musical impact across the American landscape. When young Americans saw and heard the Brits, they were shocked. The Brits' hair was long by American standards—the average American male youth had the "Peter Gun" look, and hair below the top of the ear was strange and outlandish. Likewise, their English language clashed with our mode of speaking English. For young people, especially young girls, it was a thrill of a life time to see these bands sing, play, and speak. They fell head-over-heels for the Beatles, Herman's Hermits, Yardbirds, and many other English bands.

Yet within the confines of the Hudson River enclave, acappella took off like a roaring lion. Street corner vocal groups sang the songs popularized by their favorite groups, such as The Crests, Five Satins, Penguins, Moonglows, Jesters, and many others. They sang these songs acappella, and the songs gained air time on the radio. No sooner did this happen than record labels began to sprout like wildflowers in grass. The early pioneers and founders of these records labels were less than a dozen, but acappella managed to make its music heard. Before long, live acappella shows were introduced in theaters in New York and New Jersey to full houses. Long lines of young people waited outside the theatres to hear their favorite groups. Young people pushed and shoved to be the first in line so that they could get the best seats at the front of the theater. Owners of bars, clubs, and banquet facilities hired group acts to perform for their clients. As acappella music continued to grow, TV and radio shows hosted groups, who shared their experiences with listeners. Shows were produced by icons such as the late Richard Nader in Madison Square Gardens. The late Ronnie I, founder of United Group Harmony Association, held monthly shows featuring classic R&B and acappella groups. All of the above fueled fans of the musical genre and made the popularity of acappella group singing grow immensely. Sadly, many periodicals seldom wrote about the acappella movement if they did at all. They were never mentioned in periodicals like Time Magazine, Newsweek or Billboard Magazine. Local newspapers hardly ever mentioned what was going on in the local neighborhood when it came to doo wop acappella if they did at all. They did not make it in the print media because it was an insular movement of city dwellers. So, in the end it never got the publicity it needed to expand, and go beyond its local and regional location.

As a new provincial sound, acappella was off and running, and nothing was going to stop it. It was the sound of the community, the neighborhood, the barrio. For the first time, the Hudson Sound competed with other musical regional sounds, and with the music produced by major record labels. Young people bought acappella records at record shops, and record collectors stashed them away for future gain. Acappella was moving quickly among those who loved the Rhythm and Blues group sound of the 1950s. These groups brought their songs before the public, and songs such as *"16 Candles," "Daddy's Home,"* and *"Gloria"* could be heard on the radio in acappella fashion. Young people grooved on the sound as something different and totally new. Radio stations, live shows, record shops, and clubs were all involved in this phenomenon. These acappella groups and independent acappella record labels were growing in popularity, and everyone was grooving. Before long, radio stations such as WBNX, WNJR, and WHBI played acappella recordings made by various groups who sought to gain a bigger audience. The unexpected increase in the popularity of this new musical style exploded.[34] A new art form of singing was introduced to the already crowded multitude of classification styles as acappella joined the ranks of other categories competing for a fan base, and exposed a new style of singing to the public at large. Acappella artists were living in the shadows of the big music makers, and began to compete with them. The following are some early pioneer acappella record labels:

TIMES SQUARE RECORDS	**RELIC RECORDS**
CANDLELITE RECORDS	**MEDIEVAL RECORDS**
CATAMOUNT RECORDS	**CAT TIME RECORDS**
MELOWMOOD RECORDS	**SNOWFLAKE RECORDS**
OLD TIMER RECORDS	**SIAMESE RECORDS**
HARLEQUIN RECORDS	**AMBER RECORDS**

The music makers of today are radio personalities, vocal groups, pundits, record collectors, educators, vintage record business owners, authors, and individuals who promote the group sound. Two individuals who have personified love for vocal group singing are the educators and promoters Dr. Charlie and Pam Horner. Dr. Horner's organization Classic Urban Harmony is a megaphone for group harmonization and acappella.[35] Today, this organization is the premiere promoter of the classic group sound and acappella. Thanks to the Horner's and his organization, the Hudson Sound is promoted as a viable historic sound. Their organization has made its core objective to promote, preserve, and educate the public about classic Rhythm and Blues group singing. Their mission also includes the promotion of acappella singing groups. The Horner's keep the music alive with lectures, workshops, articles, documentaries, and radio interviews. By way of example, they

---

34 https://www.vocalgroupharmony.com/TIMESSQ/Squire.htm.
35 http://classicurbanharmony.net/.

were the very first to organize an all-acappella R&B doo-wop concert at the Knauer Performing Arts Center in June of 2018 in West Chester, Pennsylvania—to a full house. They are in high demand, and anyone who is interested in learning about their work should contact them.

Another personality who has contributed immensely to the group doo-wop sound is radio personality Bob Davis. He has hosted a variety of black musical forms on his show. As an educator of black history and music, he knows the pulse and cultural trends of music. His radio broadcast is oxygen to his listeners. He continues to be a voice and megaphone for the Afro-American experience. His YouTube channel (see below) is an informative inspiration to all. Seriously consider viewing his channel and donating to his cause so that Bob can continue his work.[36]

(Courtesy Davis archives)

---

36 https://www.youtube.com/watch?v=YtvBiaPYXPY&t=48s.

WAYNE STIERLE, PIONEER AND MUSIC MAKER
(Courtesy Stierle Archives)

The music makers of the first wave of vocal group revival (1963–1973) brought synergy, tenacity, and vision to their work. They laid the foundation for future acappella singers. The music makers featured below produced their own record labels against all odds and obstacles. All of these visionaries were under twenty-five years of age, and transformed the record industry. They fortuitously created a new business enterprise within the record industry, not knowing that they were the first assembly ever to construct such an endeavor. The result was the production and manufacturing of commercial acappella recordings. Moreover, these young people created a new regional sound in the eastern region of the Atlantic coast. Although they may have been despised by record scions for their lack of business knowledge, recording engineering aptitude, and coaching skill, they had a tremendous impact on vocal group singing and its preservation. Below, you can find a partial list of those who stepped up to the plate, did their own thing, and created a groove in Vinyl City.

ABRAHAM J. SANTIAGO

ACAPPELLA MUSIC MAKERS AND CONTRIBUTORS
IRVING "SLIM" ROSE

WAYNE STIERLE

ABRAHAM J. SANTIAGO

STAN KRAUSE

EDDIE GRIES & DONN FILETI

ABRAHAM J. SANTIAGO

BOBBY MILLER

THE HUDSON SOUND

BILL SHIBILSKI

ANGELO POMPEO

Please note that many record labels produced acappella commercial recordings during the 1960s and beyond.[37] Not all of these record labels are featured here. Some labels recorded groups and then disappeared for a variety of reasons. Some labels did not produce quality recordings, since many used a 2-track recording system at the time. Keep in mind that many others made contributions unknowingly by way of their expertise, musical understanding, and appreciation of the group sound. Such individuals include Sal Donnarumma, Phil

---

37 Abraham J. Santiago and Steven J. Dunham, *Acappella Street Corner Vocal Groups: A Brief History and Discography of 1960s Singing Groups* (Glencoe, IL: Mellow Sound Press, 2006).

Rossano, Jeff Rose of Amber Records, Jerry Greene, Steve Piva, and Jared Weinstein. These individuals helped to validate R&B acappella group singing as unique, and helped to craft the Hudson Sound.

Larry Chance and Glen Fisher
Doo-Wop Revival & Doo Wop Ramblings Newsletter
WJCT- Sunday 10PM
(Courtesy Fisher Archives)

FIRST ACAPPELLA REVUE IN NEW YORK

The Five Sharks	The Destinaires
The Notations	The Rue-Teens	The Delicates
The Meadowbrooks	Joel & Concords
The Five Chancells	Chris & Cytations
The Valids	The Rituals	The Concepts
The Shadows	The Rondells	The Splendids
The Del-Capris	The Apparitions

PLUS OTHER GREAT ACTS   M.C.'S - BOBBY MILLER, PHIL ROSSANO

RKO FORDHAM THEATRE
FORDHAM ROAD & CONCOURSE BRONX, N.Y.

APRIL 12TH · TUES. NITE

Show Starts 8:30 p.m.
Everybody Welcome   All Seats $2.00

A MUSIC MAKERS RECORD SHOP PRODUCTION

TICKETS AVAILABLE AT:
MUSIC MAKERS 333 E. FORDHAM RD. BRONX, N.Y.
RKO FORDHAM BOX OFFICE
TIMES SQUARE RECORDS 63 W. 42nd ST. N.Y., N.Y.

(Circa 1966)

KEEPING THE SOUND ALIVE

PARTY OF FIVE
(Courtesy Calamito Archives)

ABRAHAM J. SANTIAGO

A PERFECT BLEND
(Courtesy ClassicUrbanHarmony.Net)

MIKE & PAULETTE MILLER
(Courtesy Miller archives)

ABRAHAM J. SANTIAGO

RELATIVES BY APPOINTMENT
(Courtesy Ziffer archives)

CHARLIE & PAM HORNER
(Courtesy of Classic Urban Harmony, LLC)

ABRAHAM J. SANTIAGO

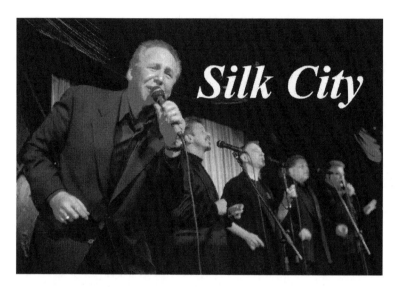

The Larkings
(Courtesy Torres Archives)

ABRAHAM J. SANTIAGO

SOUL STICK Q

Nota
(Courtesy Calrican Archives)

Patty and Val Shively
(Courtsey Shively Archives)

R&B RECORDS
THE "OLDIES" CAPITOL of the WORLD
OLD RECORDS BOUGHT & SOLD 610 352 · 2320

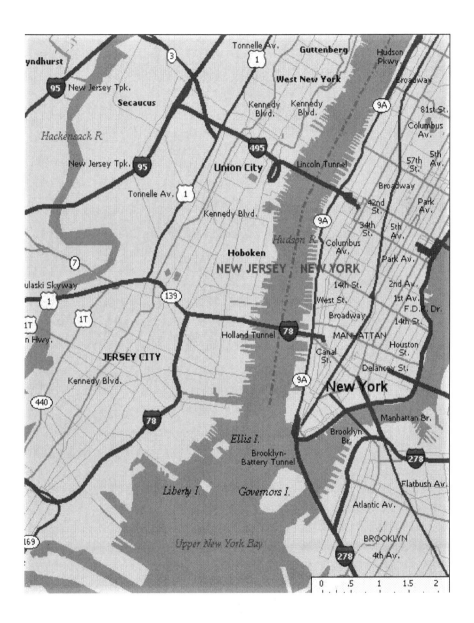

ABRAHAM J. SANTIAGO

Recording Engineer Jim Reeves with Ryan Black and Friends

jim@reevesaudio.com
EVANSTON, ILLINOIS
Tel: 847-328-6703

Abe, Tommy, Joe and Stan in his record shop
(Courtesy Santiago archives)

PART SIX
REFLECTION

CHAPTER SIX

SOMETHING TO THINK ABOUT

At the beginning of this book, it was noted that many young people were looking for meaning and purpose in life. It was likewise noted that the roots of group singing can be traced to African Americans, as well as far back to the Renaissance period. Young people sought a way to connect with one another, and searched for direction in their lives. Some found themselves drawn to music, which led to their lifelong vocation. However, for some, the search was beleaguered with minefields, obstacles, and disappointments. Many did not find what they sought to give them real meaning in life. There were those who were involved in music, but for some reason, there was always an addendum to their lives. The industry was not all glamor or freedom, by any means. For the most part, drugs, wild sex, and failure to be paid were the industry rule. There was betrayal, disease, poor hygiene, and a host of other problems. These issues came with the culture and trade craft of music that was prevalent at that time. For many, the music industry marked a slow ride downhill rather than upward mobility. Yes, money was made, but most young adults did not know the music business, and they were the victims of greedy record labels, stolen songs, and unpaid royalties.

The managers who represented vocalists and bands were double-dealers, and were looking out for themselves rather than the singers they represented. Lawyers gouged band members, singers, and vocal groups. It was an upside-down world of music in the 1960s and the years ahead. Some owners of record labels used their power to seduce or force female singers to have sex with them, as has been uncovered in R&B singer R. Kelly today.[38] Many groups and entertainers spent decades in the music field, and have nothing to show for it. These artists didn't plan their lives, because they didn't know how or didn't care to do so. They never learned a trade or skill, most never attended college to safeguard against the possibility that their music might not work out. Those who were innovative and determined and who had not earned a degree or mastered a trade craft began a start-up business in the event music might fail them, such as Patti LaBelle. In other words, many did not have a *Plan B* as a hedge. Countless singers were living for the moment. They were ripped off, and now all they have is their past, the albums they made, the celebrities they sang with, and the world tours they performed. Many never won an award like a Grammy or were inducted into a music Hall of Fame, even though the public praised these groups as great entertainers. Countless groups owed their mangers and record companies money, as this was a tactic used by the music business to refuse to pay these artists. The labels told artists that they were in debt for the recording sessions, clothes, and hotels involved in their work. Sadly, the practice of not paying singers has continued into the new millennium.[39] These entertainers have celebrity status of sorts, but have little to show for it. They are largely forgotten. Young people of today's Generation Z and Millennials have never heard of these great bands, singers, songwriters, and vocal groups of the past. The information they receive about these individuals, and others like them, are short sketches in the form of a bio, word-of-mouth, a footnote, a documentary film, or perhaps a book. The Baby Boomer generation had its own problems to cope with, but had nothing to replace these issues. Here are two examples. The 1970s were the decade of *me-ism*. Young people lost their love, and words were hyphenated, such as self-esteem, self-assertion, and self-image. In the 1980s, youth lost

---

38 https://www.nytimes.com/2019/01/04/arts/music/surviving-r-kelly.html
39 Abraham J. Santiago, *The Untold Story United Group Harmony Association* (Mellow Sound Press, 2014), pp.44.

their hope, and were fearful of epidemic diseases such as Ebola and AIDS. Today, young people have lost their ability to reason and think rationally, and are lost in a world of cyberspace and race and gender pandering. They have internalized their world, and the end result is emotional immaturity, ignorance, irrational behavior, and despair. What does this have to do with music?

What we compose, play, and sing is a direct result of our worldview and cultural trends. It reflects what we believe and who we are. For example, listen carefully to the song *"We Are All God's Gift to the World,"* sung by Jerry Lawson and Talk of the Town. The lyrics reveals Lawson's worldview. In contrast, listen to the song *"When the Party's Over"* by The Latinos. Both groups have great voices and solid harmonies and arrangements, but different worldviews.[40] Vocal group harmonization, which we inherited from our Afro-American brothers and sisters, has its roots in the realm of the spiritual. Religious elements gave African Americans hope during slavery. Their songs offered them relief from their lives of bondage. They had no musical instruments to play when they were in the fields picking tobacco and cotton or digging holes for irrigation. All they had was their voices. When they sang in acappella fashion, they sang songs of praise and comfort to their creator. The music makers of the 1950s and early 60s did something different that led to a new musical sound.

Keep in mind that the 1960s were a time of protest, free speech, and free love. The music and the Civil Rights Movement of Afro-Americans were rooted in the Christian gospel, which transcends culture, race, and religion. The vast majority of black Civil Rights leaders were Christian clergy, celebrities, students, and politicians also took part in the movement. Vocal group singing in America by people of color greatly influenced our perception of spirituality. For example, The Edwin Hawkins Singers' big hit, *"Oh Happy Day,"* which was released

---

40 https://www.youtube.com/watch?v=yIFvuAFC1mA-.
https://www.youtube.com/watch?v=rn77Yq6-OR4.

in 1969, had everyone hand clapping with the lyrics, "When Jesus washed my sins away." The song was performed live by a quartet of female singers with a male singer as background vocals and Hawkins as lead vocalist.[41]

Another example is the 1969 hit song by the 5th Dimensions, "*Let the Sunshine In/Aquarius.*" Although not a Christian song by any means, as it is a New Age song, the song did introduce spirituality to those who were looking for meaning in life. Some have suggested that the 1960s were not rooted in anything spiritual at all, and that there was no religious element to the period. Those who take that position do not know their history, and the burden of proof is on them to prove otherwise. The 1960s was a spiritual movement of Jesus, New Age, Eastern Mysticism, the God is Dead Movement, and everything in between. For example, even the standard classic song sung by so many acappella vocal groups, "Gloria," could be easily taken as a religious Christian expression. Pitilli, in his book *Doo-Wop Acappella: A Story of Street Corners, Echoes and Three-Part Harmonies* states the following:

But perhaps it is the name itself "Gloria" that drew the attention of all of those street corners serenaders… The name or word "Gloria" is sung in many religious services… [42]

For example, Hindu Indian gurus came to the West to introduce their spirituality of meditation, yoga, and communal living. Indian music was introduced to the West by artists such as the sitar player Ravi Shankar, and young people were drawn musically and spiritually to this music. However, in the end, some of their basic questions about life were never answered, such as the origin of life, morality, meaning, and destiny. The end result is that today, popular music is obscene, violent, and disrespectful to others. Many popular artists call women bitches and hos, and call men n*****s, crackers, or honky. This is due to our changing worldview and our capitulation to its norms.[43]

---

41 https://www.youtube.com/watch?v=xpXCm6U0H6s.
42 Ibid, pg.182.
43 http://www.playlistresearch.com/history/offensivelyrics.htm.

It is a fact that when a society or culture pushes a certain abnormal or deviant behavior constantly over a period of time, that negative behavior becomes the norm. In other words, that behavior gains momentum in society, and the public capitulates to the negative or objectionable behavior, thus changing the behavioral norms of the past. We can see this clearly in the contemporary worldview, as behaviors and attitudes have changed significantly in the past sixty years. It is a true indicator of our changing culture and society.[44] This change has impacted our music. For example, consider the birth of Soul music. The African American community viewed the transformation of Gospel Music in the 1940s into a non-spiritual and secular art form as an affront to the black community. Turning something spiritual that reflects the messiahship of Jesus into something secular was considered extremely offensive.

In the eyes of many people of color, the behavior of those who wrote, sang, and played that kind of music was offensive. However, this behavior eventually became acceptable to black Americans. Part of this groundswell of changing behavior comes from film, academia, and from

---

44 Emile Durkheim, *On Morality and Society*, edited and with an introduction by Robert N. Bellah (Heritage of Sociology Series, 1973), pg. 300.

our post-Judeo-Christian worldview. There was a time when people would read what Emily Post dictated about social behavior and proper etiquette. Today, that era is gone forever—as people would say today, its "old school," just like the music of the 1960s.[45] In the end, changing worldviews in music were to be expected, and people now accept the vulgarity of Hip Hop as normal. It is interesting that political correctness does not play a large part in contemporary Hip Hop or Rap. The profanity, misogynist lyrics, racist expressions, and vulgarity of these musicians are never challenged. Artists such as Snoop Dogg, Travis Scott, and J. Cole are not called out, but instead get a pass. Why is that?

Today, we can see how negative cultural norms have trickled into our music. This has also affected our social manners. Children elevate and honor those who tarnish their parents' reputation, and give these individuals celebrity status on social media outlets such as Facebook. Children abandon their parents and refuse to connect with them or call or visit them. These attitudes and behaviors have increasingly become more bizarre. By way of example, Washington State University is now providing free menstrual products in men's bathrooms.

The decision to install women's products in men's restrooms on campus is but one of a number of moves the university is making to "improve the transgender community experience on campus."[46]

Today, we accept this as normal, when it was once considered abnormal behavior. Consider, for example, the exhibits of scatological art in prestigious museums all over the world. Scatological art is art that deals with human waste and body fluids. This type of art is now common in prestigious museums and galleries. The list can go on, and this evolving cultural worldview has effected music and other art forms such as film, theatre, and dance. Listen to today's acappella street cor-

---

45 https://www.urbandictionary.com.
46 https://www.libertyplanet.com/articles/free-menstrual-products-now-available-at-mens-bathrooms-in-wsu/.

ner groups who sing in cafés, theatres, restaurants, and other public and private places. The lyrics, if you listen carefully, are what we would call today "wholesome." They are clean-cut because of the writer's cultural worldview and the cultural values of that time period. The writers of that period wrote most of the songs from the 1940s to the early 1960s.

Consider one song that encouraged students to finish high school. Ronnie & the Schoolmates' classic song *"Don't, Don't, Don't Drop Out"* was a mild success. Up until the mid-1960s, songwriting was considered a great art guild of specialists who worked in and around New York City. When the British came to the States, songwriting changed. Singers began to write their own songs, and the songwriting industry at the Brill building in New York City plummeted. Before long, songwriters were out of a job.[47] This reinforces that culture always produces something harmful in the arts in some way. With this understanding, we must ask ourselves: What is happening in the world of music? We have become a generation that **listens with its eyes and thinks with its feelings?**[48] First, we need to realize that there is something wrong with humanity as a whole. The human race is flawed; it's not perfect, and we all make miscalculations and mistakes. Notwithstanding this is the murder of Jay Austin and Lauren Geoghegan. Jay wrote the following in his journal:

…People are bad. People are evil. I don't buy it. Evil is a make-believe concept we've invented to deal with the complexities of fellow humans holding values and beliefs and perspectives different than our own…[49]

We can see this play out in today's political and religious sphere among

---

47 Doc Pomus, *Save the Last Dance for Me.*
48 https://www.rzim.org/read/just-thinking-magazine/think-again-the-gentle-goldsmith
49 https://www.independent.co.uk/news/long_reads/isis-terror-attack-cyclists-tajikistan-holiday-jay-austin-lauren- geoghegan-a8489421.html.

almost all faiths, large and small. Yet history bears testimony that the goodness of man is not true. Wars, child trafficking, anti-Semitism, and the rise of terrorism all over the world emphasize that humanity is flawed. The things that are happening today are harbingers, from climate change to famine and disease, and this speaks clearly to our flaws and the consequences of our errors.[50] Humanity is, as some would say, damaged goods. Moreover, if we are honest, the real problem in society is ourselves. Individually, we carry upon our shoulders a burden of what the sages of antiquity called "sin." Sins could be anything, such as lying, using hyperbole to embellish a statement, stealing, or slandering someone simply because he or she was a better singer, was better looking, or had more money. All of these things have a point of reference. We live our daily lives as if there are absolutes, even though we may not believe in absolutes. The problem we have, to borrow from the ancient sages of antiquity, is *sin*, or "missing the mark."

When we realize that we cannot change our behavior or attitude, or love a person as we should, we should recognize that we need someone outside of ourselves to intervene. Denzel Washington, award-winning actor, said in his speech to graduates of Dillard University, "put God first in all things."[51] The Indian gurus from the 1960s were partially correct in that there was a void among the youth during the 1960s, and today the same void exists. However, their remedy did not require self-examination and reflection; rather, it required specific actions, foods they had to eat, and money they had to give to sustain the gurus. The same could be said of many religious groups both Christian and non-Christian. These groups took advantage of young people, held them in communes, brainwashed them, and told them that the world outside was evil. These cults performed horrible acts. Consider the Charles Manson cult family, which was influenced by music—specifically by the Beatles' *White Album*, and the song *"Helter Skelter"*:

---

50 Matthew 24:3–14.
51 https://www.youtube.com/watch?v=BxY_eJLBflk.

This music is bringing on the revolution, the unorganized overthrow of the establishment," Manson told Rolling Stone Magazine in 1970.[52]

Their worldview had a veneer of religiosity that made it attractive to the gullible. It never confronted truth, or asked the tough questions, like: "What is truth?"[53] Music is one way in which truth can be conveyed. When we examine the religious leaders of the past, such as Buddha, Mohammad or others, we find that they never claimed to be the Way, the Truth, or the Life. Yet there is one person in history who claimed to be all the above, and his name is Jesus.[54] His appearance in history, art, music, and even on the covers of Time Magazine over the decades clearly indicates something unique about his personhood. Moreover, the changed lives of people who have encountered Jesus is mind-boggling. There is something about Jesus that transforms the lives of people in all cultures, and that speaks of real change.

As we search for these basic answers of life, we can find those answers in the life and resurrection of Jesus of Nazareth with clarity. His life was a life of holiness and love for humanity. When he died on the cross for our sins, he exemplified his commitment to us, and that he loves us and wants the best for us. Keep in mind that vocal group harmonization in the Rhythm and Blues style via acappella has its origin in the Christian Gospel. In light of this fact, it is worth considering examining Jesus of the Bible and be in harmony with God.

---

52 https://www.rollingstone.com/culture/culture-features/charles-manson-how-cult-leaders-twisted-beatles-obsession-inspired-family-murders-107176.
53 John 18:38, KJV.
54 John 14:6, KJV.

WORK CITED

Abraham, Santiago and Steven Dunham. Acappella Street Corner Vocal Groups A Brief History and Discography of 1960s Singing Groups. Glencoe: Mellow Sound Press. (2006).

Altschuler, G. All Shook Up. New York: Oxford. (2003).

Anthony, De Curtis and Holly George Warren. The Rolling Stone Illustrated History of Rock & Roll. New York: Straight Arrow. (1992).

Anthony, Gribin and Matthew, Schiff. Doo Wop- The Forgotten Third of Rock 'n' Roll. Iola: Krause Publishers. (1992).

Anthony, Gribin and Matthew, Schiff. The Complete Book of Do-Wop. Iola: Krause Publishers. (2000).

Arnold Shaw, *Honkers and Shouters: The Golden Years of Rhythm and Blues* (New York: Macmillan, 1978).

Awkward, M. Soul Covers. Durham: Duke University Press. (2007).

Bane, M. White Boy Singin' the Blues. Dallas: Penguin Books. (1982).

Baptistas, T. Echo of Rhythm and Blues Era. New Bedford: TRB Enterprizes. (2000).

Bell, C. East Harlem Remembered: Oral Histories of Community and Diversity. Jefferson: McFarland & Company. (2013).

Betrock, A. Girl Groups. New York: A Delilah Book. (1982).

Bradley, D. Understanding Rock 'n' Roll. Bristol: Open University Press. (1992).

Bruce, T. The Death of Right and Wrong. Roseville: Prima Publishing. (2003).

Burns, G. Jazz a History of America's Music. New York: Afred A. Knopf. (2000).

Cahill, T. The Gift of the Jews. New York City: Nan A. Talese. (1998).

Cahn, J. (2011). The Harbinger. Lake Mary: Charisma Media/Charisma House Book.

Dávila, A. Barrio Dreams: Puerto Ricans, Latinos, and the Neoliberal City: Berkeley: University of California Press (2004).

Deke, Sharon, Ben Spalding and Brody McDonald. A cappella. Alfred Music. (2015).

Dubois, N. The History of Times Square Records. New York: Lulu. (2007)

Duchan, J. Powerful Voices The Musical and Social World of Collegiate A Cappella. University of Michigan Press. (2012).

Emerson, K. Always Magic In The Air. New York: Penguin. (2005).

Evans, M. Ray Charles The Birth of Soul. London: Omnibus Press. (2005).

Floyd, A. The Power of Black Music: Interpreting Its History from Africa to the United States. New York: Oxford University Press. (1995).

Friedwald, W. Jazz Singing: America's Great Voices From Bessie Smith To Bebop

And Beyond. New York: Da Capo Press. (1990).

Goff, J. Close Harmony: A History of Southern Gospel. University of North Carolina Press. (2002).

Goosman, S. Group Harmony: The Black Urban Roots of Rhythm and

Blues. Philadelphia: University of Pennsylvania Press. (2005).

Goria, P. They All Sang on a Street Corner. Port Jefferson: Phillie Dee Enterprises, Inc. (1983).

Haralambos, M. Soul Music. New York: Da Capo Press. (1974).

Hoffmann, F. Encyclopedia of Recorded Sound. New York: Routledge. (2005).

Kelly, S. Behind The Curtains: Friesen Press. Victoria, BC (2011).

Keys, J. Du Wop. Chicago: Vesti Press. (1991).

King, J. What Jazz Is: New York: Walker Publishing Company. (1997).

Leight, A. The Vibe History of Hip Hop. New York: Three Rivers Press. (1999).

Lepri, P. The New Haven Sound. New Haven: United Printing. (1977).

Leslie, Alexander and Walter Rucker Jr. Encyclopedia of African American History. Santa Barbara: ABC CLIO. (2010).

Leszczak, B. Who Did It First? Great Rhythm and Blues Cover Songs and Their Original Artists. Scarecrow Press. (2013).

Martin, G. Making Music. William Marrow and Company, Inc. (1983).

Mellonee V. Burnim and Portia K. Maultsby. African American Music: An Introduction. 2nd ed. New York: Routledge. (2015).

Molina, R. Chicano Soul. La Puente: Mictlan. (2007).

Neal, M. What the Music said: Black Popular Music and Black Popular Culture. New York: Routledge. (1999).

Nisenson, E. Blue The Murder of Jazz. Da Capo Press. (1997).

Pitilli, L. Doo Wop Acappella: A Story of Street Corner, Echoes, and Three-Part Harmonies. Rowman & Littlefield Group (2016).

Propes, S. Golden Oldies A Guide to 60's Record Collecting. Radnor: Chilton Book Company. (1974).

Pruter, R. Doowop. The Chicago Scene. Urbana and Chicago: University of Illinois Press. (1996).

Rojek, C. Pop Music Pop Culture. Cambridge: Polity Press. (2011).

Rosalsky, M. Encyclopedia of Rhythm & Blues and Doo-Wop Vocal Groups. Lanham: Scarecrow Press. (2002).

Rudinow, J. Soul Music. Ann Arbor: The University of Michigan Press. (2013).

Santiago, A. The Untold Story United Group Harmony Association. Glencoe: Mellow Sound Press. (2014).

Santiago, J. Abraham Acappella Living in the Shadows 1963-1973: A Social History (Harbinger Press, 2016).

Schwartz, D. Start and Run Your Own Record. Label: Billboard Books. (1998).

Serrano, B. Puerto Rican Pioneers in Jazz, 1900-1939: Bomba Beats to Latin Jazz. Bloomington: iUniverse. (2015).

Southern, E. The Music of Black Americans –A History. New York: W.W. Norton & Company, Inc. (1997).

Szatmary, D. Rockin' In Time. Upper Saddle River: Prentice Hall. (1996).

Talalay, K. Composition in Black and White: The Life of Philippa Schuyler. New York: Oxford University press. (1995).

Tate, G. Everything But the Burden-What White People Are Taking From Black Culture. Broadway Books. (2003).

Toynbee, J. Making Popular Music. London: Arnold Publishers. (2000).

Tracy, S. Hot Music Ragmentation, and the Bluing of American Literature. Tuscaloosa: University of Alabama Press. (2015).

Vantoura, S. The Music of the Bible Revealed: Bibal Press. (1991).

Warner, J. Just Walkin' In The Rain: The True Story of Johnny Bragg & The Prisonaires. Renaissance Books. (2001).

Warner, J. American Singing Groups. New York: Billboard Books. (1992).

Whitburn, Joel Top *R&B Singles, 1942-1999* (Menomonee Falls, Wis.: Record Research, 2000).

Whiteis, D. Southern Soul-Blues. Urbana: University of Illinois Press. (2013).

ABOUT THE AUTHOR

Abraham Santiago is a bestselling author, music historian, and vocal group enthusiast for over fifty years. He was once a former disc jockey in California on station KCSS 91.9 FM during the early to mid-70s. He is also a film producer and songwriter. His music has appeared on PBS in 2001 in the Emmy Award winning documentary film "American High", by producer J.R. Cutler. Santiago was a vocal group member of The Concepts during the 1960s acappella era. He is the recipient of The Best Book Award by Soul Patrol.com in 2006 with co-author Steven J. Dunham. In 2011, his film "Street Corner Harmony" was a nominee for Best Documentary Film at The Golden Door International Film Festival in Jersey City, New Jersey. For speaking engagements contact him at: msproductions66@yahoo.com

APPENDIX

HARMONY WITH GOD

Gospel music in which R&B emerged has always had a spiritual connection. The Afro-American experience is rooted in the hallowed union to the God of Abraham. This spiritual link displayed itself in many vocal styles, and it has always been associated with the God of heaven. It is in this context, that the God of the Holy Bible reveals himself through natural disasters, government upheavals and personal experiences. The experience of many people who have gone through trials and hardships has led them to repent and to trust in the living God of Israel. By genuine repentance and faith alone in Messiah Jesus, mankind can reconnect with the living God and have peace and harmony.

PEACE AND LIFE

God loves you and wants you to experience his PEACE. Since it was God's plan for us to experience peace, purpose and direction in our lives, why is it that most people have not experienced it?

"For I know the plans I have for you," declares the LORD, "plans to prosper you and not to harm you, plans to give you hope and a future. Then you will call upon me and come and pray to me, and I will listen to you. You will seek me and find me when you seek me with all your heart."

Jeremiah 29:10-13

SEPARATION FROM GOD

God created us to have a relationship with Him and to experience all that he has for us. He loves us just the way we are and accepts us for who we are. Yet, we have a choice to accept Him or reject Him. Unfortunately, our desire is to please ourselves. This choice created a separation from God.

"I have no peace, no quietness; I have no rest, but only turmoil."

Job 3:26

GOD'S REMEDY

God has provided the remedy. Therefore, we must make a choice.

"Come now, let us reason together, says the LORD. Though your sins are like scarlet, they shall be as white as snow; though they are red as crimson, they shall be like wool."

Isaiah 1:18

RECEIVE THE MESSIAH JESUS OF NAZARETH

Man is sinful and separated from a HOLY GOD. Sin results in a lack of purpose, direction, and peace. Only through Jesus can we receive forgiveness of SINS.

"Jesus answered, "I am the way and the truth and the life. No one comes to the Father except through me."

John 14:6

Repentance and faith alone in Jesus is the only way we can be in HARMONY WITH GOD. It is not through being good, giving to charity or attending religious services.

"The fool says in his heart, there is no God. They are corrupt, their deeds are vile; there is no one who does good. The LORD looks down from heaven on the sons of men to see if there are any who understand, any who seek God. All have turned aside, they have together become corrupt; there is no one who does good, not even one."

Psalm 14:1-3

"Or do you show contempt for the riches of his kindness, tolerance and patience, not realizing that God's kindness leads you toward repentance? But because of your stubbornness and your unrepentant heart, you are storing up wrath against yourself for the day of God's wrath, when his righteous judgment will be revealed. God will give to each person according to what he has done."

Romans 2:4-6

What is keeping you from experiencing his forgiveness and being in harmony with God?

INDEX

A

acappella
  birth of, 19, 24
  definition, 16
  founder of, 72
  group members, 21
  movement, 43
  record labels, 25, 74
  singers, 19
  Soul, 34
  style, 12
  Vocal group singing, 12–13, 16
Acappella Record Labels
  Amber Records, 74
  Candlelite Records, 74
  Cat Time Records, 74
  Catamount Records, 74
  Harlequin Records, 74
  Medieval Records, 74
  Melowmood Records, 74
  Old Timer Records, 74
  Relic Records, 74
  Siamese Records, 74
  Snowflake Records, 74
  Times Square Records, 74
acappella vocal groups, 35, 43, 107
all-acappella R&B doo-wop concert, 75
America baritone-conscious, 34
Austin, Jay, 110

B

Baby Boomer generation, 105
Barrett, Richard, 22
Beach Boys, 3
Bellah, Robert N., 108
Big Brother, 3
black Civil Rights, 106
Black, Ryan, 100
black/Puerto Rican, 41
Blue Notes, 25
Booker T, 7
Both Sides Now, 10
British Invasion, 72
Brooklyn group, 27
Brunswick Records, 6

INDEX

Butler, Jerry, 6

C
Catamount label, 43
Champagne Pop, 4
Chance, Larry, 87
Charles, Ray, 17, 34–35, 114
Chi-Lites, 6
Chicago Sound of Illinois, 6
Christian clergy, 106
Christian gospel, 106, 112
Christian song, 107
Civil Rights Movement, x, 106
Classic Urban Harmony, 74, 93
Cole, J., 109
Collins, Judy, 10
Colon, Willie, 8
Comin In on a Wing and a Prayer, 20
Cooper, B. Lee, 24
Countless groups, 105
Countless singers, 105
Crawford, Candice, 43–44
Cream, 3
Crosby, 33–34

D
Daddy's Home, 73
Davis, Bob, 75
Davis, Carl, 6
decade of me-ism, 105
Dells, 6
Denver, John, 9
Diddley, Bo, 6
Dogg, Snoop, 109
Don't, Don't, Don't Drop Out, 110
doo-wop acappella, 16, 43, 107
Durkheim, Emile, 108

E
Edwin Hawkins Singers, 106
epidemic diseases, 106
Epstein, Mortimer, 57, 60

F
Fania label, 7
Fania Records, 7
Fileti, Donn, 81
Fisher, Glen, 87
Folk Sound, 10
Funk Band, 6

G
Geoghegan, Lauren, 110
girl groups, 43, 113
Gloria, 73, 107
Goldblatt, David, 24

INDEX

Gordy, Berry, 6
Gorsset, Gus, 18
Gospel Music, 108, 119
Green Onions, 7
Gries, Eddie, 81
Guy, Buddy, 6

H
Harlow, Larry, 8
Harold Melvin, 25
Helter Skelter, 111
Hold on I'm Coming, 7
Holding Company, 3
Horner, Pam, 74, 93
Humanity, xi, 56, 110–112

I
I Dug Acappella, 20
I Got a Woman, 17
If I Had a Hammer, 10
Impressions, 6
It Must be Jesus, 17

J
James J. Ferris High School, 56, 61
Jazz players, 6
Jefferson Airplane, 3
Jesus, 17, 107–108, 112, 119–120

Jive Five, 35
Judeo-Christian worldview, 109

K
Kelly, R., 22, 105
King, Carole, 53
Knauer Performing Arts Center, 75
Krause, Stan, 18, 22, 25, 38, 80, 113

L
LaBelle, Patti, 105
Latin record label, 7
Lawson, Jerry, 27, 34, 106
Let the Sunshine In/Aquarius, 107
Little Anthony, 24, 35
Lymon, Frankie, 35, 41

M
M.G.'s, 7
Maestro, Johnny, 24
Manson, Charles, 111
Marrow, Helen, 57, 59
Masucci, Jerry, 7
Mayfield, Curtis, 6
Millar, Bill, 19, 23
Miller, Bobby, 20, 82

INDEX

Moore, Sam, 7
Motown Records, 25, 46
multi-layered country, 3
musical regional sounds, ix, 73
musical sounds, 2, 8, 12, 45

N
new millennium, 26, 46, 105
1950s acappella (LP), 26, 34
Nota, 26, 97

O
Oh Happy Day, 106
Okeh label, 20
Old Timer Records, 20, 74
On Morality and Society, 108

P
Pacheco, Johnny, 7–8
Palmieri, Eddie, 8
Philadelphia International
  Records, 25, 46
Philla Sound, 7
Picket, Wilson, 33
Pitilli, Lawrence, 16, 107, 115
Pompeo, Angelo, 84
Prater, Dave, 7
prominent vocal groups
  Autumns, 35

Del Capris, 35
Five Jades, 35
Heartaches, 35
Savoys, 35
Psychedelic Rock, 3, 6

R
R&B singer, 105
Redding, Otis, 7
regional sounds, ix, 2, 7, 10, 73
Religious elements, 106
religious leaders, 112
Renaissance period, 16, 104
Robinson, Smokey, 6, 26
robust psychedelic rock, 6

S
Salsa, 7–8
Santiago, Abraham J., 13, 41, 46, 84, 105, 118
Scatological art, 109
Scott, Travis, 109
Shankar, Ravi, 107
Shibilski, Bill, 83
Shively, Val, 98
Sins, 107, 111–112, 120
Sitting on the Dock of the Bay, 7
16 Candles, 73
"Slim" Rose, 16, 22, 72, 78

INDEX

social-cultural revolution, 3
soul music, 6, 108, 115–116
SOUL STICK Q, 96
Soulful Singers
    Notations, 34
    The Chessmen, 34
    The Royal Counts, 34
Sparks, Randy, 10
Stax Memphis sound, 7
Stax Records, 7, 25, 46
Stierle, Wayne, 18, 21–22, 25–26, 77, 79
Supremes acappella, 25

T

Take Me Home, Country Roads, 9
The Concepts, 64, 67, 118
The Connotations, 42
The Del Capris, 66
The Emeralds, 43, 65, 67
The Five Fashions, 45–46
The Five Sharks, 45
The Heartaches, 63
the Imperials, 24, 35
The Larkings, 95
The Latin Kings, 66
The Medallions, 28, 64
The Memphis Sound, 7

The Miracles, 6
THE PENGUINS, 28, 30
The Persuasions, 27, 34, 47
The Surfing Sound, 3, 6
the Teenagers, 35, 41
The Untold Story United Group Harmony Association, 46, 105, 116
The Valentines, 65
This Land is Your Land, 10

U

upside-down world, 104
urban folk, 13

V

Vinyl City music, 25
Vinyl records, xi, 11, 71
Vocal group harmonization, 16, 106, 112

W

Washburne, Christopher, 8
Washington, Denzel, 111
Waters, Muddy, 6
We Are All God's Gift to the World, 106
Wexler, Jerry, 20

When Jesus washed my sins away, 107
When the Party's Over, 106

Y
young people, 2–3, 7, 10–11, 21–25, 53, 72–73, 77, 104–107, 111

Made in the USA
Columbia, SC
07 September 2019